CITIZENS AND THEIR GOVERNMENTS
Rights and Values

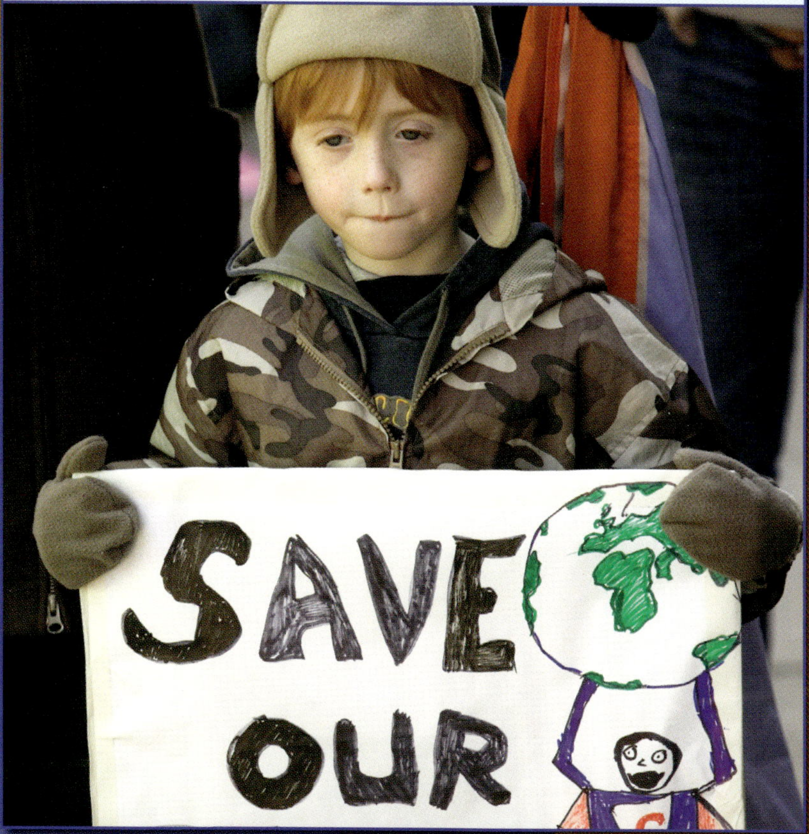

Patricia Hynes

Cherry Lake Publishing
Ann Arbor, Michigan

Published in the United States of America by Cherry Lake Publishing
Ann Arbor, MI
www.cherrylakepublishing.com

Cover, © Ashley Cooper/CORBIS; Title Page © Ashley Cooper/CORBIS; Page 7, Photo Courtesy of Library of Congress; Page 22, © David Turnley/CORBIS; Page 26, © Frances G. Mayer/CORBIS

Copyright ©2008 by Cherry Lake Publishing
All rights reserved. No part of this book may be reproduced or utilized in any form or by any means without written permission from the publisher.

Library of Congress Cataloging-in-Publication Data
Hynes, Patricia Freeland.
 Rights and values / by Patricia Freeland Hynes.
   p. cm.—(Citizens and their governments)
 Includes index.
 ISBN-13: 978-1-60279-065-0
 ISBN-10: 1-60279-065-5
 1. Civil rights—United States. 2. Constitutional amendments—United States. 3. United States. Constitution. 1st-10th Amendments. I. Title. II. Series.
 KF4749.H96 2008
 342.7308'5—dc22   2007006087

Cherry Lake Publishing would like to acknowledge the work of
The Partnership for 21st Century Skills.
Please visit www.21stcenturyskills.org for more information.

TABLE OF CONTENTS

CHAPTER ONE
The Foundation of Our Government — 4

CHAPTER TWO
The Bill of Rights — 7

CHAPTER THREE
The Bill of Rights in Action — 13

CHAPTER FOUR
When There Is No Bill of Rights — 20

CHAPTER FIVE
Safeguarding Our Rights — 26

Glossary — 30

For More Information — 31

Index — 32

CHAPTER ONE

The Foundation of Our Government

The very first—and largest—words on the U.S. Constitution describe all of us: "We the People."

We often hear that, as citizens of the United States of America, we enjoy rights that we should value. We may be reminded that earlier Americans fought to gain and keep these rights.

Just what are these rights? Who grants them? Why are they so valuable? How do they apply to everyday life? The answer is in the **Constitution** of the United States and the **Bill of Rights**.

When it was written, the United States Constitution outlined the basic principles by which the new nation was to be governed. These same principles still govern us today.

For example, the Constitution divides power among the **executive, legislative,** and **judicial** branches. Ours is a government of, by, and for the people. It was unique in the 1700s when the nation was founded. Since then, many other nations have used it as a model.

At the time the Constitution was created, the Revolutionary War had recently been fought to free America from English control. How do you think many of the English viewed this new country and its Constitution?

The ancient Greeks developed an early form of democracy. This was especially true in the city-state of Athens. In Athens, only men who owned land or their own homes could vote. How is the American system different?

The Constitution was **ratified,** or agreed to, in 1789. At that time, it became law. Almost immediately, those who had drafted the document made additions to it. Their purpose was to make sure that certain rights for individuals were clearly spelled out. Doing so would make it harder to take away these rights in the future.

CHAPTER TWO

The Bill of Rights

James Madison, who was the fourth president of the United States, has also been called the "Father of the Constitution."

The result of the effort to clearly spell out rights was the first 10 **amendments** to the Constitution. We call them the Bill of Rights.

Some 17 more amendments have been added since then. A proposed amendment must be ratified by a majority of the states within a specified amount of time. Let's look at the Bill of Rights. The next four pages describe each of the 10 amendments.

Amendment 1

People shall have the right to their own religion, to freedom of speech, and to assemble, or meet in large groups. People shall also have the right to complain about the government and to speak out in "the press," including newspapers, magazines, TV, books, etc.

Every week, millions of Americans attend religious services of their choice.

The right to speak out is protected by the Constitution.

Amendment 2

People can own and keep guns.

Amendment 3

The government can't have soldiers live in people's homes except in time of war and only then if Congress passes such a law.

Amendment 4

The police and others must get an OK in the form of a search warrant from a judge before entering or searching a person's home.

Amendment 5

People accused of crimes must be convicted in court or set free. No person can be taken to court a second time for a crime for which he or she has been found not guilty.

The right to own guns carries with it the responsibility to use those firearms responsibly.

The Constitution sets out ways to make all trials fair.

Amendment 6

A person accused of a crime is entitled to a prompt trial. The accused person must be told what he or she is accused of. The person is entitled to be in the room when witnesses testify against him or her.

Amendment 7

An accused person is entitled to a trial with a **jury**.

Amendment 8

An accused person cannot be made to pay an unnecessarily large **bail**.

Amendment 9

The people have many rights. Some are listed in the Constitution, but others are not.

Amendment 10

The powers not given to the federal government by the Constitution or prohibited to the state still belong to the states and the people.

Americans cherish the rights that the Constitution gives them.

CHAPTER THREE

THE BILL OF RIGHTS IN ACTION

Over the years, the rights guaranteed in the U.S. Constitution have influenced millions of trials nationwide.

The Bill of Rights was added to the Constitution on December 15, 1791, when the Constitution itself was just one year old. More than 200 years have passed since then. The rights that the Constitution grants and the

The Supreme Court has been very careful to protect the right to free speech. Can you think of a situation when it should *not* be protected?

issues it raises are as important today as they were in the late 1700s. Here are just a few of the modern examples of those rights.

Freedom of Speech

During the Vietnam War, three students in Des Moines, Iowa, wore black armbands to school. John Tinker was 15, and Christopher Eckhardt was 16. John's sister Mary Beth was just 13 years old. When the three wore their armbands, they were suspended from school. The case, called *Tinker v. Des Moines,* went to the Supreme Court. In 1969, the court decided that the students' First Amendment right to freedom of speech had been violated.

Freedom of Religion

Amish people believe their religion tells them to live apart from worldly influence and that education should end after eighth grade. However, many state laws say children must go to school until they are 16. In a case called *Wisconsin v. Yoder,* the Supreme Court decided in 1972 that the First Amendment right to freedom of religion was more important than Wisconsin's desire for all its citizens to have two more years of school.

Protecting the rights of groups such as the Amish is also the responsibility of the state and local governments. What kinds of situations might arise on the local levels?

After the 9/11 terrorist attacks, some people said that the government should be allowed to spy on citizens. They argued that people who had not done anything wrong had nothing to worry about. Do you agree or disagree with this position? Why?

Protection Against Unreasonable Searches and Seizures

In 1957, police in Cleveland, Ohio, received a tip about a criminal suspect at the home of Dollree Mapp. Police went to the house and entered without a search warrant from a judge. The police didn't find a criminal suspect, but they did find other materials that they believed were against the law. Mapp was convicted of having these materials, but the Supreme Court said the conviction was wrong. In 1961, the Court ruled that since the police did not have a search warrant, nothing they had found could be used against Mapp.

The Right to a Lawyer

In 1961 in Florida, Clarence Earl Gideon was charged with burglary. When the case got to court, he asked for a lawyer, but Florida law did not provide for that. Gideon represented himself, and he was convicted. Finally, the Supreme Court reviewed the case. The Court ruled that the Sixth Amendment had been violated because Gideon had not been able to have a lawyer represent him. Gideon got a new trial and was found not guilty.

After he was sent to prison, Gideon used the prison library to help him write about his case to the Supreme Court. Gideon's persistence and hard work paid off. The Supreme Court agreed to review his case.

21st Century Content

Today, all police officers in the United States must tell suspects of their rights because of this case. This is known as the "Miranda warning." However, this is not the case in many countries.

The Right Against Self-Incrimination

In 1963, Ernesto Miranda was arrested in Arizona. Police asked him many questions, and Miranda confessed. At his trial, Miranda's confession was the only evidence against him, but he was convicted and sentenced to jail for up to 30 years. The Supreme Court said that because of the Fifth Amendment, the confession could not be used against Miranda. The police had not told him that he did not have to confess. Miranda got a new trial.

One good test of the value of the Bill of Rights is that it has not become outdated. Remember, when the Bill of Rights was written, there were no airplanes, cars, TV, radio, cell phones, or Internet. People used horses to get around. Only white men who owned property could vote. However, this remarkable 200-year-old document has successfully guided us as we look for modern answers to modern problems.

As you review the Bill of Rights, ask yourself this question: How would it be different if it was written today?

CHAPTER FOUR

When There Is No Bill of Rights

Peaceful protests such as this one are rare in some nations outside the United States.

Sometimes it is easy for Americans to forget that people in other nations don't always have the same freedoms they do. These freedoms are precious. Too often in the past—and even today—people around the world have been denied these freedoms. However, many people everywhere keep fighting for these rights.

The Right to Speak Out

Throughout much of the 1900s, the hundreds of millions of people in the old Soviet Union had to be very careful about everything they said. Speaking out against the government was very, very dangerous, and the government had many spies. People said, "The walls have ears."

The government owned all the newspapers, and the radio and TV stations. News reporters never said anything bad about the country. However, people knew that things were very bad, indeed.

As leader of the Soviet Union, Joseph Stalin was a dictator. He had millions of people killed for political reasons. What are some safeguards against this happening in the United States?

Despite the violent reputation of the Soviet Union's government, its collapse and later failed coup were largely without bloodshed.

The Right to Assemble

In the early 1990s, the people of the Soviet Union rose up against their government. Even though they didn't have a Bill of Rights to protect them, they decided to change things. They held huge protests in the streets. Even when soldiers and tanks appeared in the streets, the people didn't go home in fear. Instead, the Soviet Union collapsed. It broke into 15 separate countries. The people were free!

A Failing Effort

The people of the Soviet Union were able to get their government changed. They gained the right to assemble and to speak out. Others have not been so lucky. Among them are the billion people of China.

On April 15, 1989, college students in Beijing held a strike in memory of a government leader who had supported democracy. When a newspaper reported that the students were causing trouble, more students joined them in Tiananmen Square.

Tiananmen Square was built more than 500 years ago when an emperor ruled China. The huge space covers 1,443,000 sq.feet (440,000 square meters). Today, many tourists like to visit, some remembering the 1989 events.

Tiananmen Square is an enormous space that has been the symbolic center of China for centuries.

On May 4, about 100,000 students, workers, and just plain citizens held a march in support of democracy and freedom of the press. Soon protests began across the country. Eventually, there were protests in about 400 cities. On the night of June 3, soldiers and tanks stormed into the thousands of people in Tiananmen Square. As many as 5,000 people may have been killed. The protest was over. The government of China would not allow freedom of the press and democracy.

The events in Tiananmen Square were shown on TV all over the world. Ask your parents and grandparents what they remember and their thoughts about China at the time.

CHAPTER FIVE

SAFEGUARDING OUR RIGHTS

In the 1800s, George Caleb Bingham painted *County Election,* in which white males—frontiersmen—form two lines. In one line, they cast their votes. In the other, they begin to celebrate. The painting suggests that the voters have chosen the candidate who pays for the party. This is not

Bingham painted County Election *in 1851–52 and showed white male farmers, shop owners, and others voting.*

a very positive view of our form of government! Unfortunately, in some cases in the past, it was probably accurate.

Today, the painting may have a sort of charm. We are so far away from this part of our past that it may now seem romantic. However, voting **fraud** is not romantic. It was a serious crime then and still is today.

You can begin early to protect voting rights. Some organizations allow young people to serve as interns at polling places. Interns learn how the process is supposed to work and how to be sure it does.

How do people vote in your community? Do people vote on paper ballots or some other way, such as on electronic voting machines? You might be interested in reading arguments for and against electronic voting machines.

The U.S. Constitution and Bill of Rights give Americans the right to worship when, where, and how they wish.

Your Rights and Responsibilities

Think of what you have just learned about the U.S. Constitution and the Bill of Rights. Because of these documents, you have the right to read and say whatever and meet with whomever you choose. You have the right to vote for your government leaders. You have the right to go to the church, mosque, synagogue, or whatever house of religion you choose. You have the right to be protected in court if you are accused of a crime.

Study the past. Learn about the present. Continue to explore your rights under the Constitution, the Bill of Rights, and the other amendments. With this background, you will be better able to understand current events. You will become a responsible participant in American democracy. You, too, will cherish the freedoms that other Americans hold so dear. The Twenty-Sixth Amendment lowered the voting age to 18, so your time to become a voter is coming faster than you think!

The Statue of Liberty in New York Harbor represents the freedom of Americans to people around the world.

Glossary

amendments (uh-MEND-muhnts) official alterations or additions to a document

bail (beyl) sum of money exchanged for the release of an arrested person as a guarantee of that person's appearance for trial

Bill of Rights (bil uv rahyts) name given to the first ten amendments to the U.S. Constitution

Constitution (kon-sti-TOO-shuhn) written document that describes the nature, functions, and limits of government

executive (ig-ZEK-yuh-tiv) one of the three branches of the U.S. government; this branch is made up of the president of the United States and his or her delegates

fraud (frawd) something done on purpose for unfair or unlawful gain

judicial (joo-DISH-uhl) one of the three branches of the U.S. government; this branch is made up of the federal court system, including the Supreme Court

jury (JOOR-ee) small group of citizens chosen to hear evidence in a trial and decide guilt

legislative (LEJ-is-ley-tiv) one of the three branches of the U.S. government; this branch is made up of Congress

ratified (RAT-uh-fahyd) approved or formally accepted

For More Information

Books

DeVito, Anne. *A Kids' Guide to the Bill of Rights: Curfews, Censorship, and the 100-Pound Giant.* New York: HarperCollins, 1999.

Nardo, Don. *Opposing Viewpoints in World History: The Creation of the United States Constitution.* Detroit: Greenhaven Press, 2004.

Medina, Loreta M., editor. *Turning Points in World History: The Creation of the United States Constitution.* Detroit: Greenhaven Press, 2003.

Jordan, Terry L. *The United States Constitution and Fascinating Facts about It.* Naperville, IL: Oak Hill Publishing, 1999.

JusticeLearning.org. *The United States Constitution: What It Says/What It Means: A Hip Pocket Guide.* New York: Oxford University Press, 2005.

Other Media

Go to *http://pbskids.org/wayback/civilrights/features_suffrage.html* to learn more about the fight for women's right to vote.

To find out more about the U.S. Constitution, go to *http://www.usconstitution.net/constkids4.html*

Play the Bill of Rights game at *http://www.constitutioncenter.org/explore/ForKids/index.shtml*

To find out more about the Bill of Rights, go to *http://www.citizenbee.org/user/* from the Bill of Rights Institute.

INDEX

Amendment 1, 8, 14, 15
Amendment 2, 9
Amendment 3, 9
Amendment 4, 10
Amendment 5, 10, 18
Amendment 6, 11, 17
Amendment 7, 11
Amendment 8, 12
Amendment 9, 12
Amendment 10, 12
Amendment 26, 29
amendments, 7
Amish, 15
Arizona, 18
arms, 9
Athens, 6

bail, 12
Bill of Rights, 5
  explanation of, 8–12
  history of, 4–6, 13–14
  Supreme Court and, 14–18
  value of, 19, 28
Bingham, George Caleb, 26–27

China, 23–25
Constitution of United States, 5
  amendments to, 7–19, 29
  ratification, 6
  separation of powers in, 5
County Election (Bingham), 26–27
court, 10, 11
democracy, 6
  in Greece, 6

Eckhardt, Christopher, 14
England, 5
executive branch of government, 5

Florida, 17
fraud, 26–27
freedom of press, 24
freedom of religion, 8, 15
freedom of speech, 8, 14, 28
freedom to assemble, 8, 22–23

Gideon, Clarence Earl, 17
Greek democracy, 6
guns, 9

Iowa, 14

judicial branch of government, 5
jury, 11

legislative branch of government, 5

Madison, James, 7
Mapp, Dollree, 16
Miranda, Ernesto, 18
"Miranda warning," 18

9/11 terrorist attacks, 16

Ohio, 16

police, 16, 18

ratified, 6
religion, 8, 15
Revolutionary War, 5
right against self-incrimination, 18

rights
  to assemble, 8, 22–23
  to bear arms, 9
  Bill of Rights, 4–6, 7–19
  in China, 23–25
  free press, 24
  free speech, 8, 14, 28
  to a lawyer, 17
  in other countries, 20–25
  religious rights, 8, 15
  in Soviet Union, 21–23

search warrants, 10
self-incrimination, 18
Soviet Union, 21–23
spies, 21
Stalin, Joseph, 21
Supreme Court, 15, 16, 18

television, 25
Tiananmen Square, 23–25
Tinker, John, 14
Tinker, Mary Beth, 14
Tinker v. Des Moines, 14
trials, 10, 11

U.S. Constitution, 5

Vietnam War, 14
vote
  age for, 29
voting fraud, 26–27

Wisconsin, 15
Wisconsin v. Yoder, 15

ABOUT THE AUTHOR

Patricia Hynes grew up in Pennsylvania, where she climbed hills and trees and swam in the local river. She attended college in Pennsylvania and got a degree in literature and secondary education. In both high school and college, her writing was published in school literary journals. She has spent her adult life teaching and writing for young people and has lived in Baltimore, Boston, Chicago, Florida, and Canada. She now lives in Venice, California, with her husband, a painter and dentist, and a fluffy orange cat named Stinky.